JUMBO SHRIMP &

Other Almost Perfect Oxymorons*

*Contradictory Expressions
That Make Absolute Sense

JUMBO SHRIMP &

Other Almost Perfect Oxymorons*

*Contradictory Expressions That Make Absolute Sense

Warren S. Blumenfeld, Ph.D.

A PERIGEE BOOK

Perigee Books
are published by
The Putnam Publishing Group
200 Madison Avenue
New York, NY 10016

Back cover photograph by John Disney © 1986 by Georgia State University

Library of Congress Cataloging-in-Publication Data

Blumenfeld, Warren S.
    Jumbo shrimp & other almost perfect oxymorons.

    "A Perigee book."
    1. Oxymoron—Anecdotes, facetiae, satire, etc.
I. Title.   II. Title: Jumbo shrimp and other almost
perfect oxymorons.
PN6231.W64B5   1986   428.1′0207   86-16950
ISBN 0-399-51306-X

Typeset by Fisher Composition, Inc.

Printed in the United States of America
1 2 3 4 5 6 7 8 9 10

Acknowledgments:
Blameless Culprits
and/or
Unsung Heroes

It would be easier to acknowledge those incredibly few, but **tremendously small,** people who didn't encourage me; but that would be **oxymoronic logic.** Rather, let me attempt the more difficult, albeit the more pleasant—to acknowledge, with genuine appreciation, the many who did encourage me, did make positive contributions:

Hermann Remmers (a master teacher from whom I am still learning).

Ken Olshan (who gave me my first opportunities to publish—and humor at that).

Steven Kutner, Herbert Kaufman, and Norman Sanders (all of whom kept me, and keep me, in the game).

Several people I never met and whose names I'll never know (two of whom are in my sight at all times).

Milton Blood (who put me in the oxymoron closet).

David Snell, Vickie York, Herschel Brown, Billy Bowles, Mark Donovan, and Adrienne Ingrum (all of whom brought me out of the oxymoron closet—even if only on a **permanently temporary** basis).

Students, faculty, and staff at Georgia State University, citizens of Atlanta, and citizens of non-Atlanta (so many of whom let me know it was a crowded, albeit cavernous, closet).

Lamar York (who thinks I may know how to pronounce "oxymoron" correctly and increased my vocabulary by one word—or approximately 5%).

Pat Andrews, Norman Arey, Sandra Carnet, Ginger Carter, Mike Feldman, Joan Hamburg, George Harris, Paul Harris, Wayne Herman, David Hop, Ange Humphrey, Dave Kosloski, Yetta Levitt, Shelby Loosch, Ron McKeen, Bruce McMillan, Nancy Neill, Lisa Nicholas, Bill Oliver, Thomas Oliver, Chuck Podhaisky, Tom Pynn, Mike Rosen, Peter Tilden, Mike Wade, Liz Wickersham, and Chip Wood (all of whom let me hone my interview guest skills at **real potential** risk to their professional careers as media talent).

The 1986 Georgia House of Representatives, particularly Peggy Childs, John Russell, and Paul Bolster (all of whom managed to **essentially agree** about **oxymoronic worth,** thereby demonstrating great **political promise**).

Josh Blumenfeld and Esther Blumenfeld (both of whom put up with this **important trivia** long before it was either).

Loyce McCarter (all of whom knew).

Anna Jardine (without whom I would have broken all known rules of style and grammar—many intentionally).

Lisa Amoroso (whose patience is exceeded only by her artistic talent).

People who write, read, speak, and/or listen . . . and college students and/or teenagers (for **obscurely obvious** reasons).

All are **special—but in the same way.** If I have inadvertently left anyone out, it is only because I meant to.

To myself, without whom I **definitely probably** might never have done whatever it is I seem to have done here.

In addition, however, to my mother (whence cometh my sense of humor, such as it is), who is both funny and a lady. Ergo, hi, Mom.

Also, hi, Esther, Josh, **and/or** Loyce.

And to Mrs. Richardson, who demonstrates **old age** can be an oxymoron.

Thanks, all; you deserve better.

Grandchild

Contents:
Random
Organization

Clean dirt

Forgive me if I sound like a professor; but in point of fact, truth be told, that's what I am—at least that's what my contract says. Indeed, a **full professor**—and that just may be an oxymoron.

This book (so-called) is **slightly preoccupied** with oxymorons. Oxymorons. I am never sure whether I need to define them or defend them. It is rather like playing trivia (albeit **important trivia**). If you know the answer, it is not trivia; if you don't know the answer, it is trivia—a true dichotomy with no "in between." (Some would, perhaps convincingly, argue that it is trivia either way. I certainly hope so. But I won't argue the point. I'll leave it up to you.) Therefore, fully aware of the possibility of insulting at least one group of readers—although I am not sure which, the group that does know about oxymorons, or the group that does not—let me begin with pronunciation and definition. (You see, old professors, and habits, die hard.)

PRONUNCIATION
It usually embarrasses me that I always mispronounce the word "oxymoron." Don't you mispronounce it. It is pronounced roughly the way it looks and sounds. (Antepenultimists—go ahead, look it up—be warned.)

DEFINITION
An oxymoron is two concepts (usually two words) that do **not** go together but are used together. It is the bringing together of contradictory expres-

sions. Consider **jumbo shrimp** (please!), **freezer burn, even odds, divorce court, near miss, cardinal sin, good loser, slightly pregnant, Amtrak schedule, civil war,** and **clean dirt.**

Oxymorons are an addictive (remember, you heard it here) semantic phenomenon that traditional English literature has systematically overlooked—or at least treated with **intense apathy.** Admittedly, oxymorons are slightly lower than puns on a prestige scale. They are the Rodney Dangerfield of our language—perhaps deservedly so. They don't get no respect; but then, they don't deserve no respect. They are hardly an **open secret,** their **obvious subtlety** notwithstanding. (And with **feigned apologies** to Henny Youngman, they are short one-liners.)

UBIQUITOUS AND INSIDIOUS

Further, unintentional and/or intentional use of oxymorons is growing. What has come to be known as "weasel wording" is closely akin to oxymorons. This "copping-out" behavior increasingly used by, among others, those who write and/or speak, is a **veiled apparent** attempt to say everything to everybody that ends up **saying nothing** to anybody—however eloquently.

ON BECOMING ADDICTED: A **BRIEF ODYSSEY**

I first came across the label **oxymoron** during a time when, for personal physical reasons (my vision was impaired), I had more time to think than I cared to—as well as less time to pursue my industrial-organizational psychology teaching and research interests than I cared to. I had been **vaguely aware** of the phenomenon for years; but it was not until an esteemed colleague (whom I will **definitely probably** never forgive) gave me the label for the phenomenon that I began systematically to collect (and, forgive me, catalog) oxymorons. They were indeed insidious; I found them all the time, everywhere—just as, unfortunately, you will from this day henceforth.

Once my awareness level had heightened (as yours now has), I was surrounded—and **justifiably paranoid**—about them. **Almost suddenly,** I noticed that on one wall in my office was posted a wonderful Robert Frost quote describing a person as being **completely educated.** Some of my file drawers were labeled **completed research.** I realized I was talking about **standard deviations,** as well as **normal deviates,** in class. And how about **manic-depressive**? A trusted colleague came from a department called **Criminal Justice.** Was a **love-hate** relationship evolving, closing in on me? Further, I was not alone in this particular semantic closet; the interest was there. (Gasp!) Could I rise **above principle**? Could I walk away a **mini-winner?** Alas, addiction, where is thy sting?

A few years ago I was selected by students, faculty, and administration at Georgia State University as the College of Business Administration alumni distinguished professor. (Should I have been flattered or insulted? Had I been damned by **faint praise**? Or feinted by **damn praise**?) In the course of the activities that followed, I developed a professional and a social relationship with our public information director. Aha, I figured (incorrectly, as it turned out), a chance to use all the resources of this mighty university to gain visibility for my varied behavioral research (presumably not an oxymoron) interests in such things as document readability, performance measurement, selection (particularly performance prediction via biographical data), job attribute preferences, interrater reliability, training evaluation, experimental design, the use of item analysis, discriminant analysis, factor analysis—along with other rare and exotic univariate and multivariate statistics. But no, it was not to be.

At first to my bemusement, and subsequently to my dismay, the thing that interested the public information director was none of the above erudite behavioral research applica-

13

tions. Rather—and I should have anticipated this—because he was a **wordsmith,** he was interested in my (then) **casually intense** interest in oxymorons.

He was hooked, addicted (as **approximately 102.60%** of you soon will be). I was the **semantic pusher.** Soon, not unlike junior high school kids, we were exchanging oxymoronic notes, then phone calls (our wives and secretaries threatened to take away our telephone privileges—inter alia). It soon became impossible (but **extremely unimportant**) to discern who was the addicted and who was the pusher.

One day he called to tell me he had arranged an interview for me with a writer from one of the Atlanta newspapers. At last, a chance to make my research visible, I figured again—and incorrectly, as it turned out. The interview took place. I was totally prepared regarding my research interests. Unfortunately, I made the mistake of mentioning oxymorons. The resulting article dealt only with oxymorons. To make matters worse, the writer understood the concept. He titled the article **"Clever Professor."**

The mail literally began pouring in, not requesting research reprints, as professional egos (not necessarily an oxymoron) demand, but offering additional oxymorons, thanking me for putting a label on the phenomenon readers had also observed (gotcha?), asking where they could find more oxymorons (gotcha!), was there a clearinghouse (gotcha again!), and so on.

A few weeks later, the editor of our faculty/staff monthly called me. She had been told about me and my oxymorons. She had seen the newspaper article. Would I consider writing a column? I suspected before that I was **somewhat addicted** to oxymorons, but I now knew I was hooked. There was little or no point in fighting the problem.

Appropriately humble, I began writing the column. In addition to drawing from my oxymoron file, I invited readers to participate. (Do you see it coming?) The response was such that the column eventually essentially **wrote itself.** Many folks were repeaters, oxymoronic recidivists, if you will. It became the read badge of courage to get published in the column. Interdepartmental squabbles were aired. Someone in the Marketing Department submitted **management science.** To which someone in the Management Department shot back **marketing research.**

I ran a **first annual** plural-of-oxymoron survey. Official alternatives were (a) oxymorons, (b) oxymora, (c) oxymori, (d) other, (e) other other, and (f) other other other. I even set a **first deadline!** (The winner came in fifth; and I'm still **certainly unsure** of the correct plural of **oxymoron**—but then I probably couldn't pronounce it anyway.)

In the interim, no one remembered (or cared, apparently) about my research. With **cavalier concern,** I **insincerely vowed** to kill the column at quarter's end; but it wouldn't die. It was becoming a **science fiction** creature, taking over my life with **glacierlike rapidity.**

OXYMORONIC VISIBILITY

Too late. I received a phone call from the editor of a neighborhood newspaper asking if I would write a similar column. **Almost totally** crushed, and not knowing whether to laugh or cry, I did so for several months. Mercifully, the newspaper folded **(no pun intended),** although by all editorial accounts (and mail) it was the readers' favorite column. The editor even considered trying to keep the newspaper alive by asking me to increase the column size and frequency. I declined—flattered, but **clearly confused.**

Many people correctly perceived the oxymoronic condition of our country. My interest in oxymorons was subsequently described in *Business Atlanta.* I did local radio call-in shows. I did a "straight" interview with a Canadian radio science magazine. I even made several **academic presentations** on oxymorons as a communication barrier.

I made a presentation on oxymorons at the Third International Conference on Humor (apparently it had happened at least twice before). Then it happened.

To be **almost candid,** a feature interview with the Atlanta *Journal & Constitution* was greeted with widespread indifference. However, another feature interview with the *Detroit Free Press* was picked up on the Knight-Ridder wire service; and the oxymoron mail kept coming. (Would you believe an editorial—**for and against** oxymorons—in the Wichita *Eagle and Beacon*?)

People magazine contacted me to do an interview. It was a delightful experience. One of the senior editors came to Atlanta. We planned to spend two hours on the interview, but **perhaps predictably,** he was so fascinated with oxymorons we spent six. The magazine subsequently flew in a photographer from Maine (no, not packed in ice). For a day and a half, he became part of the family as film exposure followed film exposure. (It is entirely possible that none of us in the family will ever be able to smile again!)

After the *People* feature, I had opportunities to do several radio **talk shows** across the country. As a result of those opportunities, there are still, I guess, several oxymoron contests going on. I have also done some **live television** (or maybe it was the other way around). To date, the only network television I've done is with WTBS (Atlanta Superstation), a program fortuitously called ***Good News.*** Here in Atlanta people refer to WTBS as the local network. (Yes, **local network** is . . .)

I received coverage in *The Korea Times (Chicago Edition),* a 99% + foreign-language newspaper. Noting my **resolute ambivalence** regarding this turn of events, my mother reminded me it was altogether fitting and/or proper I should be covered in the Chicago edition—inasmuch as I was born in Chicago. The woman has a fantastic memory! And obviously bears little or no grudge.

Then, to add injury to insult, I was accorded the **minor honor** (which I accepted with **arrogant humility**) of having the Georgia House of Representatives pass a resolution (H.R. No. 953, dated 7 March 1986) commending me—in spite of my more traditional scholarly pursuits—for my interest in oxymorons. It concluded by recognizing me as the

"Novice Master of Oxymorons." They sent me **three originals** (as distinguished from **original copies**). Again, I didn't know whether I should laugh or cry. Of **minor moment,** however, is the fact that the resolution **certainly probably** was the only thing the legislature agreed upon that whole session—possibly. **Positively grudgingly,** I wrote the resolution sponsors a thank-you note, allowing **political promise** was one of my favorite oxymorons.

THE **EXQUISITE PAIN** OF IT ALL

I feel very much the **semi-perfect idiot savant** (yet another delightful, albeit scientific, oxymoron). It would be accurate to say response to my oxymoronic activities may be characterized as having moved with **deliberate speed** from **intense apathy** to **mild interest** to **partial success** to **controlled enthusiasm,** finally even approaching **qualified success** (be still, my heart). And I sincerely hope all this will not result in **artistic success** (an oxymoron rivaled only by **academic salary**). **Semi-honestly,** I need the money: Not only am I an admitted **semantic pervert, gregarious recluse, linguistic flasher, curable romantic, cynical idealist, full professor, conservative liberal,** and **former tall person,** but my wife is a **full-time free-lance professional writer,** and my son has declared an **undecided major** in college—this semester.

All these activities I submit as evidence of latent widespread interest in this semantic backwater called oxymoron. Where have I gone wrong? Was it something I said? After all, this is **serious humor**!

18

Routine emergency

Purpose and Organization: **Planned Serendipity**

*T*he single purpose of this **first annual** book is to describe the ubiquitous and insidious nature of oxymorons, to raise your awareness level about oxymorons, to infect and/or addict you, TO RUIN YOUR LIFE, just as mine has been **somewhat destroyed.** Fair warning: Those of you who enjoy being human may want to forget everything you have already learned, try to return this book, and ask for your money back. The rest of you may wish to press on—your **faulty logic** and **sound judgment** notwithstanding.

FOUR POINTS

If you are among those who got this far, my **extensive briefing** has already raised (and that is not intended to be a homophone) your awareness level. (If you are part of the **minor majority** who didn't get this far, put this literary gem down immediately, if not sooner!) In the **too few** pages Putnam has generously allotted, I will address four points in pursuit of my **capriciously avowed** purpose of mass oxymoron addiction. (Oxymoron OD?)

First, I'll show you how to semi-distinguish between true and quasi oxymorons. Next, I'll start you on your very own personal search for the ubiquitous and insidious oxymoron. Then, I'll describe the **chaotic organization** of this **relatively definitive** compendium. And, finally, I'll provide a means for **semantic sanity**—use it; you'll need it.

TRUE OXYMORONS VERSUS QUASI OXYMORONS

With **sincere apologies** to a classic textbook on behavioral research methodology, I have found it helpful to classify oxymorons as either true or quasi. To the best of my knowledge, this is not an official classification scheme but, rather, one I have coined—and one that works for me. Try it; I'll like it.

A true oxymoron is a contradiction in a natural state, independent of personal values. Examples of "trues" are **almost perfect, bittersweet, eloquent silence, sweet and sour, fast food, thunderous silence,** and **sweet sorrow.**

A quasi oxymoron is, by definition, not a true oxymoron. (Why didn't you think of that?) It *is* characterized by personal values and, perhaps **best or worst** of all (depending on one's values), includes an **element of sarcasm.** Examples are **military intelligence, legal brief, Texas chic, faculty cooperation, sophisticated New Yorker, educational administration,** and (forgive me, Adrienne) **compassionate editor.** Some might argue—convincingly, unfortunately—**oxymoron expert** is an oxymoron (but not me!). Quasis are most people's favorites; but I like them anyway (quasis—not most people).

If you have a problem distinguishing trues from quasis, you are probably human.

OXYMORON SOURCES

I am **always occasionally** asked by **interested students, parking lot attendants,** or **intimate strangers,** "Dr. Blumenfeld, where can I find the ubiquitous and insidious oxymoron?" To which I reply with **hurried patience,** "Relax; oxymorons find you." Teaching someone how to find oxymorons is almost as difficult as—and surprisingly similar to, although in a different way—teaching someone to breathe. Oxymorons are to be found everywhere (occasionally intentionally); but some places are better sources than others. Therefore, I strongly recommend (with **slight qualification**) you search out situations where people write, read, speak, and/or listen. Forget about other situations; you will **almost certainly** be wasting your discretionary spare time. Failing that, try **research reports,** office memos, journals, government documents, newspapers, magazines, radio, television, **form letters,** personal letters, newsletters, marketing messages, movies, books, speeches, conversations, **understanding editors,** and **pure academe,** among others—

for openers. I am also particularly fond of *Time* magazine and reruns of *M*A*S*H* (perhaps the happiest of all hunting grounds). In short, search out oxymorons from life, and if that's too restrictive, elsewhere.

CHAOTIC ORGANIZATION
To make my task easier, and yours more difficult, the contents of this **bare treasure-trove** are **randomly organized** into the **relatively independent** categories listed on the contents page. There is also a conclusion which puts all of this into **oxymoronic perspective** (*see* conclusions, but don't peek until you get there).

If you have a problem with why a particular oxymoron is in one category rather than another, you probably are **reading and thinking—dangerously enlightened** behavior I find personally offensive. **Constructive criticism** notwithstanding, you are no doubt probably correct. And I agree; most oxymorons fit into more than one category within my perfect taxonomy. Others fit in **none or more.**

Parenthetically, I would have included other topics, but I couldn't think of any that tied together so neatly and logically. In addition, I received a **firm commitment** from the publisher they would permit me only five oxymoronic categories. So you will just have to get along with these—unless the executive editor softens her position and lets me bring out **another different definitive** compendium besides this one. That seems unlikely—given her **firm maybe** on this book. We'll see. (After all, that's the **only choice.**)

Each of the eleven oxymoron categories contains oxymorons I've found fairly recently. **Few if any** don't make at least **partial sense.**

REQUEST FOR OXYMORONIC CONTRIBUTIONS (I GAVE AT THE EDITOR'S)
Henceforth, you will find oxymorons difficult (better, impossible) to avoid. Stepping nimbly to one side just won't do it any longer. That is the ubiquitous nature of the beast. Further, you will need an oxymoron outlet.

I propose (for our mutual **mental hygiene**) we share our oxymorons. Mail in your oxymorons—ten maximum, please (see page 95). I will compare them to my files. If your oxymoron is **old news,** well and good, and **insincere thanks.** But if it is a find, even better, and **less insincere** thanks. Be sure to include the source—**self-conception** (think about it), **research reports,** office memos, journals, government documents, newspapers, magazines, radio, television, **form letters,** personal letters, newsletters, marketing messages, movies, books, speeches, conversations, **understanding editors, pure academe,** *Time, M*A*S*H*—whatever. Also indicate the category. I intend to include your contributions in future oxymoron books. (This assumes the present book gets published.)

WARNING
My **clear conscience** requires I inform you that oxymorons have almost absolutely no socially redeeming quality except that they make people **smile out loud.**

FINAL WARNING
Oxymorons are **addictive—but not necessarily habit-forming,** or in that order.

SECOND FINAL WARNING
Again, they are not for everyone—only people who write, read, speak, and/or listen . . . and college students and/or teenagers. Having salved my conscience, I leave you with this **single thought:** THINK OXYMORON. Or, as we simple folks here in **north Georgia** are wont to say, CAVEAT EMPTOR, Y'ALL.

---

[1] Some but not all oxymorons are set off in boldface. Few if any oxymorons got by me, my concerned publisher, executive editor, or copy editor. A **major minority** of you may find it of interest to see how many, if any, non-boldface oxymorons you can identify. (The **relatively few intentional typographical errors** don't count.) Be advised that (a) there are approximately 1,231 oxymorons in the book, (II) absolutely no recognition will be given to the astute reader who identifies all—or more than all—the oxymorons, and (3) no approximate solution—or even exact count—will ever be made available. Sleep well.

My first wife and I have what many describe as a **mature marriage**—possibly even a **happy marriage** (although **married life** . . .). At the time of this **book writing,** we have had **almost exactly** 25 years and 10 months of **wedded bliss**—and 25 years and 10 months out of **almost exactly** 30+ years ain't **too bad**!

However, because she recently became a full-time free-lance professional writer, her values have changed as we approach our golden years. **Functional sentiments** like typewriters, tape recorders, and file cabinets have **perhaps understandably** become more important, and are better received, than candy, cards, and flowers. A few years ago (for **her anniversary,** or maybe it was her birthday, I forget which—which didn't totally endear me to her), I gave her a two-drawer file cabinet. Given that **filing system** had become a true oxymoron (the paper seemed to be growing overnight, needing to be pruned each morning—why else would she have hired the live-in gardener?), she was **mildly delighted.** Faced with organizing herself and/or her files, she asked me to act as **creative consultant**—no doubt because of my reputation as an office organizer (my offices—particularly my **home office**—remain at gridlock).

As she left to make the final assault on our local **shopping center,** I told her to leave her newfound problem in my skilled, but capable, hands. It would be at least **partially organized** by the time she returned. After I had **deliberated roughly 20.76 seconds,** the top drawer was labeled "Miscellaneous" and the lower drawer "Other." When she returned, she was appropriately grateful. And to this day (even as we speak), her two-drawer filing system (actually a **genuine imitation** of the **functional system** at my **neat office**) consists of miscellaneous and/or other . . . and it works!

I figure if it's good enough for her, it ought to work here. Also, I thought I would begin with miscellaneous and/or other so as not to get distracted by the subsequent more systematic categories. Therefore, anyone who sees any rhyme, reason, and/or cohesion to the trues and quasis in this unit is possibly a **functional illiterate.** (Read on.)

We recently ran an oxymoron contest among the **student body** at Georgia State University. And while the winner did not come in first, there were some **first-rate oxymorons.** Attend to **diamond ring, justifiable homicide, bad sex.** Other nonwinners (or **good losers,** if you prefer) were these:

> **conventional wisdom**
> **last initial**
> **kickstand**
> **vacuum-packed**
> **closed window**
> **President Reagan**

A few summers ago, I drove my son to Boy Scout camp in **north Georgia.** During the trip, I passed a sign purporting a **Southern-style delicatessen.** As I say, I passed—hot corned beef and/or pastrami on white bread (sliced into quarters, with **fuzzy toothpicks**), a **sweet pickle,** and **warm mayonnaise**?

Texas International Airlines? **Air Atlanta**? You may recall for a time it looked as if **Eastern Airlines** might become an oxymoron. As a matter of fact, some would argue. . . .

Have we discussed **airline food**? **Casual sex**? (Casual sex!)

Historians (modern or otherwise) will **long note and little remember** the Magna Carta made **King John** an oxymoron.

See if you can find the oxymoron in the following list:

global village
normal human
true illusion
white gold
exact estimate
limited obligation
abundant poverty

Quite by accident (I assure you), I recently had reason to buy a new car. When I asked an informed salesperson what color the sporty, albeit non-sports, car was, he responded **"subtle red"** . . . and I bought it. (He was right—firemen often honk, wave, and/or follow me home.)

Traffic flow? Most cities have a cab company named **Courtesy Cab.** Don't laugh, next time you see one of their cabs; I need the advertising for the book. **Cab driver**?

Sports Illustrated said of Kareem Abdul-Jabbar's **skyhook,** "Perhaps the greatest tribute to its **complex simplicity** is that the skyhook never became a trend."

A restaurant here in Atlanta describes itself as being **casually elegant.** Does that mean I do—or don't—have to dress? And having almost nothing to do with that, *Time* magazine recently talked about **state ownership.**

Fish farm

I still have trouble with **fish farm,** as well as the following:

minor miracle
family life
distant relatives
home cooking
tragic comedy
simply superb
city park

I also remain in **minor awe** of **real magic.**

My father, with the possible exceptions of my grandfather and me, is the world's most unhandy person—although he perceives himself as just the opposite. It is traditional for him to tell us proudly he has **fixed** (whatever) **before—many times.**

For years the fatherly advice I have been giving my son (now an **older teenager** and a student at the University of Maryland) as he departs for who knows where with who knows whom to do who knows what until who knows when has been: "Have fun; and think." He is **too nice, too considerate,** to remind me my advice is **certainly oxymoronic**— although he apparently is still doing both and **may certainly** continue to do so. During his freshman year, one of the students was **elected king.** I immediately reminded him he was there to get an education, not collect oxymorons. (I had hoped the curse would skip a generation.) We have a **fairly stable** father-son relationship—although sometimes it is **almost impossible** to tell who is which.

Someone recently was described as being **too handsome** (which I suppose is better than being **pretty ugly**). On the other hand, *Sports Illustrated* struck once again, describing

Danny Manning as being **too unselfish.** But, then, he is **only talented** as well.
Once again, see if you can find the oxymoron in the following list:

tastefully gaudy

incredibly real

almost safe

happily forlorn

benign neglect

deliberately thoughtless

Oxymoronic trivia: **Georgia peaches** (they come from South Carolina).

I mentioned earlier that the *Detroit Free Press* article (entitled, by the way, "Serious Word Play: Opposites Attract Oxymoron Expert") describing my oxymoronic curse (no oxymoron, that) had been picked up by a wire service. While **almost no** copy editing was done, the local newspapers did get into the oxymoronic spirit with their retitles. Close your eyes and see if you can find the oxymorons in the following retitles:

"Collection of Oxymorons Becomes Full-Time Hobby for Psychology Professor"
   (*The Arizona Republic*)

"Oxymoron Expert Takes Humor Seriously" (*Spokane Daily Chronicle*)

"Collector of Oxymorons Has Learned to Expect the Unexpected"
   (*Home News,* New Brunswick, New Jersey)

"Collector of Oxymorons Speaks of Serious Humor"
   (*The Miami Herald*)

"Professor's Oxymoron List Is New, Improved"
(Yakima Herald Republic)

"Contradictory Phrases Give Professor a Working Hobby"
(The Jacksonville Journal)

"A Serious Sense of Humor" *(The Times-Picayune,* New Orleans)

"Some Serious Humor: Oxymorons Are Scholar's Hobby"
(Kansas City Star)

"A Terribly Enjoyable Hobby for a Professor"
(The Philadelphia Inquirer)

Rather than indulging in **excessive moderation,** I am going to bring these miscellaneous and/or other oxymorons to a **rolling stop.** If you think some of these oxymorons belong somewhere else (presumably, however, in this book), I won't argue at all—hardly. I have little or no objection to your removing an **unwanted oxymoron** (surgically if necessary) and performing your very own oxymoron transplant. Be well.

And don't feel you must be **wildly silent;** take **restrained advantage** of the form on page 95. However, I **apathetically urge** you to articulate proper placement of your oxymoron.

Working vacation

Working Vacation
and Other Business and Office Contradictions

The business world is very much with us, or against us, depending on your point of view. Don't take my word for it. Look at the business pages of your local newspaper (or **national local,** *USA Today*). Even if you don't read the business pages, other media forms (particularly television) will bring business to your attention—if not focus. Most of us are involved with business in one way or another and/or have, at one time or another, worked in an office. So **few if any** would argue **office work** is an oxymoron.

Given this common experience, I leave it to you to decide whether **business ethics** is a true oxymoron or a quasi oxymoron. Personally, I am definitely ambivalent. And who can ever forget the evergreen oxymoron **original copy**? Further, I am starting to think **working vacation** is more than an oxymoron; it is a **lifestyle.** As a matter of fact, I am beginning to suspect **business school** may be an oxymoron.

Here are some of my favorites, more or less. **No doubt** you will recognize and probably identify with most of them. They are **uncommonly common.**

It is hard to read the business pages without discovering another **friendly takeover.** True or quasi?

Want to pick an argument with your secretary? Let that person know you think **secretarial science** is an oxymoron. Or better (or worse), suggest that person thinks lunch hour is an oxymoron. (Secretaries, the appropriate response is **considerate boss**.)

A **few more** business and office oxymorons:

considerate secretary
corporate planning
office administration
statistical significance
enough resources
initial deadline

Most typists can tell you the difference between a **final rough** draft and a **rough final** draft. Would that I could. I guess I am getting old again, but I can remember when "word processor" was an oxymoron.

As an industrial psychologist (no, I refuse), I guarantee **objective rating** to be an oxymoron. Think about it. Also think about these:

parent company
management development
corporate family
production schedule
debugged program
planned change

Regarding **employee benefits,** which to some may indeed be an oxymoron, I am forced to scratch my head (or at least bring my hand to my head) when I hear **death**

Corporate family

benefits. I suppose it means something to someone (maybe even theologically)—although perhaps too late.

Almost certainly there's a special place in that great organizational chart in the sky for economists, who gave us **negative income,** (mayhap, **tax return),** and of course, that **semiannual perennial** winner, **economic forecast.**

Finally, a particularly **bittersweet** business and office oxymoron (right behind **office life**) is **office space.** And while I am as fond of **Bankers Trust** as the next oxymoron collector, I would be **almost totally** remiss without including one of my all-time favorite quasis—**zero defects** . . . and **zero deficit.**

Have I left out your favorite business and/or office oxymoron? Not to worry; give at the office. See page 95—**immediately, if not sooner.** Incidentally, **favorite oxymoron** is an oxymoron; but of course you knew that.

Back-up Forward:
Giving
Oxymorons a
Sporting Chance

*A*s **accurately reported** somewhere herein, I was born in Chicago—although I **fairly seriously** doubt it would claim me (and thanks). However, the **almost actual truth** is that my parents lived in northwest Indiana at that time. Therefore, when they decided to bring me back to our Indiana home, I became a **bona fide Hoosier** (is that the **good news** or the **bad news**?). And, for the **unofficial record,** there is little or no truth to the rumor that students here refer to me as "Indiana Blumenfeld." (Besides, what I do on weekends is my **own business**.)

The term "Hoosier Hysteria" (regardling basketball at least—particularly at the high school level) is no oxymoron. Early in this life, I learned **basketball game** (at least in Indiana) was—and is—an oxymoron, mayhap the truest.

Given the above, you can readily understand why I have considerable difficulty dealing with **professional softball;** but then, true oxymorons get to me. During a recent Kentucky Derby, the jockeys were described as **diminutive giants.** Fortunately nobody told the horses.

With the **possible single exception** of true quasi oxymorons, **classic new movies,** educational television, and the **good life,** I have **almost no** addiction problems. That includes golf. However, when I recently heard a TV announcer describe a golf club as a **metal wood** (true or quasi?), I shook my head, and tried to play through.

35

Therefore, until **golf game** becomes a non-oxymoron, take a slice at these:

secure coach
Falcon defense
full stadium
Little League
Braves fans
professional amateur
Yogi Berra language

Would anyone care to take a position on **free agent** in baseball? Don't ask me; ask the owners.

I saw an **interesting bumper sticker** the other day: "Bring professional football, baseball, and/or basketball to Atlanta." And while two out of three ain't bad, I kept on driving, not wishing to look back on the possibility something might be gaining on me and/or I might turn into a pillar of **low salt**.

A woman basketball player was recently described as a **female jock.** (Talk about functional autonomy!) I immediately pulled out my copy of *Gray's Anatomy*. Too late, she went hardship.

Have you noticed how many **sports events** are referred to as the **first annual classic**? Once again, I must have missed something. Speaking of missing, **Minnesota basketball** and **Tulane basketball** have become oxymorons, sadly. Happily, however, San Francisco basketball has returned to non-oxymoron status.

Try a **leisurely sprint** through the following:

extra tickets
organized baseball
secure manager
Braves highlights
Billy Martin tenure
football game
contractual obligation

In trying to decide whom to foul during the closing seconds of a basketball game, the team intending to foul (**intentional foul**?) had a problem—the other team had **several best** free-throw shooters. Perhaps this was **somewhat related** to the fact one player was consistently referred to as the **sixth starter**—not only an **unfair advantage,** but possibly a **close relative** of the **back-up forward.** I dribbled on, suggesting many would argue **amateur athlete** to be an oxymoron. You can pay me now, or you can pay me later.

While **systematically browsing** through cable television stations, I came across a football game between two **small college powers** in Indiana. I immediately thought the **informed sportscaster** might be Rod Serling, but no. (And no yet again; this was neither **Indiana football, Purdue football,** nor even **Notre Dame football!**) After watching for a few minutes, it became **remotely obvious** (in my **unbiased, but objective, opinion**) both teams were overmatched. However, what was of interest (to me at least, in terms of this book) was the Wabash College nickname—**Little Giants.** I suppose that's all right, as long as they stand up straight.

I also have some difficulty relating to **underpaid professional athlete—underpaid amateur athlete** perhaps, but . . .

Do the terms **World Championship of North America** or **World Championship of the United States** ever get to you? They **definitely may** now. How about **uncrowned king**?

Also, do you think **drag race** may also have overtones of a sexual identity crisis to it? Hey, no one is prefect (with the possible exception of Inspector Clouseau).

Water polo also tugs a bit at my heartstrings. Finally, trust me when I tell you I understand basketball—but a **good foul**? And I am **often occasionally** shaken by the **oxymoronically descriptive** "He plays taller than he is."

Well, sports fans, as we round third and head back to the barn, you may be thinking your favorite sports oxymoron received an **active bye**. If so, be **passively aggressive**; charge the oxymoronic ball. Use the form on page 95 to turn the game—if not the book—around.

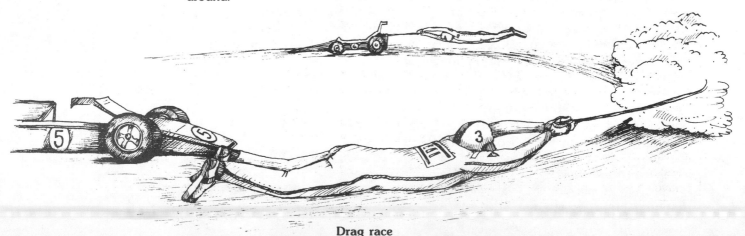

Drag race

One nice thing about being at a university with a quarter system—as opposed to a university with a semester system—is that the quarter ends. I forget the other nice thing.

Nevertheless, at least once a semester, usually during a **school vacation,** a faculty member will slip and speak his and/or her mind with **common candor, thoughtfully blurting,** "Wouldn't this be a wonderful place to work if it weren't for the damn students?" So much for **job satisfaction!** The **relative truth** of that statement notwithstanding, these oxymorons deal with education—at all levels, from graduate school up.

In a class a few years ago, I observed two students arguing. They couldn't agree, although both wanted to compromise, get it over with—and save face. Finally one said, "Everything is relative anyway." To which the other countered, "Not necessarily, it depends on how you look at it"—thereby destroying the **lesser evil,** and me, in the process. And that's how we're going to look at education—oxymoronically, as in **academic excellence** and **quality education.** You may recognize yourself, your classmates, and all your **favorite teacher.**

Teachers know it is easier, **almost pleasant,** and **educationally productive** to teach elective—rather than required—courses. Typically, students want to be there. Witness the black heel marks outside (required class) rooms into which eager students are dragged yelling and screaming. I have so far arranged to teach **elective courses.**

Academic Salary
and Other
Learned Oxymorons
from Education

39

Academic salary

I developed and **host/teach** a doctoral seminar (with the fetching title "Methodology of Behavioral Research in Organizations"). How tough is the course? Well, not only do I not take prisoners after the second meeting, but the students, in front of my back, refer to the course as a **marathon sprint,** staying away in droves—avoiding me like a summer-quarter term paper. Unfortunately, **mature students and advisors** recognize the course as critical. It is now referred to as a **required elective.** Once again, where have I gone wrong? Are you sure Mr. Chips got started this way? How about Mr. Coffee?

Try an **unwelcome recess** with the following:

student athlete

teacher lounge

academic freedom

teacher union

class monitors

high school sports

faculty cooperation

short semester

There is little or no truth to the rumor that at many engineering schools the English department is considered part of the foreign languages group—although at registration at Purdue (as at probably every engineering school in the country), there was a sign **modestly proclaiming:** "Two weeks ago I didn't know what an engineer was, now I are one."

School lunch is a truly true oxymoron (the **height of depth**). **Academic salary** will always be with us (at least up until the second week in every month). **Full professor**?

Wealthy professor? And have you ever thought about **student teacher**? Also, do a **little homework** on the following:

enough time

building fund

teacher salary

student interest

winter vacation

educational administration

productive meeting

academic humor

Scholarship fund qualifies!—everywhere. I certainly suspect **budget plan, faculty coordination, inexpensive textbook,** and **collegial respect** deserve some class time. And I have already credited Robert Frost with suggesting a person could be **completely educated.** (I'd like to meet him—the **completely educated** person, not Robert Frost.)

My high school was tough. **Student counseling** was between nonexistent and marginal at best. If you were college prep (and I was), you took wood shop rather than machine shop (and I did). I took it twice (almost). **Automotive science**?

And I think it was Mort Sahl who talked about a friend of his who majored in mid-seventeenth-century Tibetan history but was working as a bank teller until he could find an opening in his field. I understand; but it could have been worse—he could have over-specialized. Good academic advisement pays.

Nursery school? I had a group like that last quarter—and they were seniors. Every

Summer school

time you think you've heard it all, you hear two more. The other day one of my **less esteemed,** or perhaps more accurately, **unesteemed,** colleagues was described as a **terrific hypocrite.** I guess so; but first I want to hear it from him—to my face.

Incidentally, our faculty has been inappropriately maligned. In point of fact, we do have faculty who can read and write; unfortunately, it's not the same person.

There are fascinating job titles in education. What do your lecture notes **subtly reveal** regarding **associate dean, research assistant, assistant principal, academic dean, school nurse, band director,** and/or **graduate student?** Many **readable university catalogs** describe departments and courses such as **industrial relations, criminal justice, career guidance, modern history, elementary calculus, accounting history,** and **educational psychology. Final week** sounds almost theological, apocryphal, and/or terminal.

At the end of each **academic year,** faculty are wont to wish each other a **productive summer.** I pass; there's still enough of Huck and Tom in me to realize **summer school** may be the cruelest—if not the truest—**educational oxymoron.**

Many teachers consider **concerned parent** to be an oxymoron—and I'm not going to touch **PTA. Eternal truth** notwithstanding, if you feel I did not turn in your pet pedagogical oxymoron—and you seek extra credit—use the self-explanatory form on page 95. Welcome to the oxymoronic **alumni association** (hurt until it gives).

44

Fast Food
and Other Food
and Health
Oxymorons
by Which to Live

*I*nformed pollsters report the country is **somewhat health-conscious.** I qualify. Not only do I live in the country, but as indicated earlier, as **almost everybody,** I have had health problems. Recently, however, there was the **real possibility** of my having to go back to surgery. **Minor surgery**? Only when the other guy has it!

Incidentally, which is the true oxymoron? **Complete cure** . . . or **incomplete cure**?

Anyway, my **physicians agreed** I was overweight, potentially presenting surgical problems. Asked if I had been watching my weight, I replied, "Yes, I have been watching my weight; it has been going up for many years." But then, I have a short but undistinguished history in regard to this particular problem. A physician once told me my weight was perfect, but unfortunately I was too short for my height. **Moderately motivated,** for months I tried—almost successfully—to gain height. Essentially failing to do so, I sought out another physician who told me I should get back into sports. I immediately took up sumo wrestling.

So far at least, there has been a relatively **happy ending** to this story. I did not have to go back to surgery; but they did get my partial attention. I took off fifty pounds (thereby getting myself back down to a **svelte chubby**) by **speed walking.** My first wife is ambivalently fond of telling **interested strangers** I walked my ass off.

Anyway, **ill health** is a **too true** oxymoron, one of the many facts of this life.

I get a **little uneasy** when I hear about **designer water**—although not as uneasy as I do when I hear about **designer cigarettes**.

No one is ever going to describe me as being on either the front edge or the back edge of the avant-garde. Fairly frankly, I have a reputation for being **dynamically stodgy;** but don't you think **natural foods, meatless meat, odorless garlic,** and yes, **fresh raisins** are just a **little much**? I will give you **fresh yogurt,** however.

An informed acquaintance tells me there is **soy ice cream.** Okay, if you say so; but I'm going to put some **nondairy creamer** on mine, and hold the **turkey ham** (gently, if at all possible).

Do you suppose a menu exists anywhere that doesn't include **jumbo shrimp**? (I certainly hope not, he said shellfishly.) That same menu might also include **nonalcoholic beer**—but certainly not **chicken nuggets**. Mayhap **white rosé**? **White chocolate**? Do you suppose there really is a truly **dry martini**?

If you recognize the food and health oxymorons below, you are probably a **health fanatic.**

sweet and sour
fast food
baked Alaska
lasting fad
white burgundy
frozen food

I heard a radio commercial pushing a **salmonburger**—an **all-American salmonburger** at that! Not only will I pass, but I think I'll swim upstream.

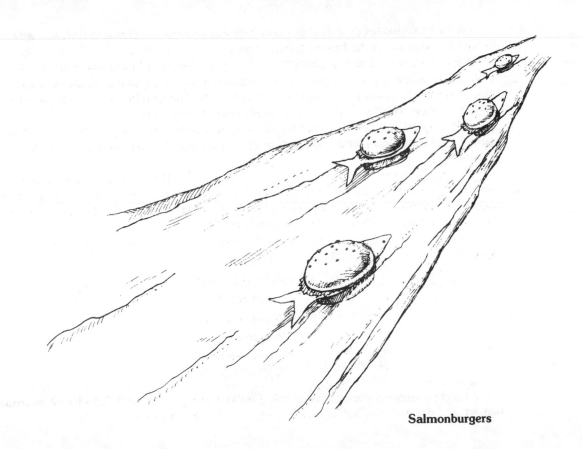

Salmonburgers

A local **weather forecaster** described the weather as being **good flu weather.** However, weather notwithstanding, as a **restrained gourmand,** I salivate wildly at the mere mention of a meal of **gourmet hamburger, plain caviar, chilled grilled** salmon, **frozen French fries,** and **inexpensive wine.** Not exactly your **Grandpa Jones special,** but . . .

Many **health plans** contain an option for dental work (no doubt **painless dentistry**) as well as our selecting the **available physician** of **our choice.** I suppose that is **medical humor,** as might be **liquid gas** and/or the following:

physical fitness

recreational drug

dry ice

complete menu

fun run

bad health

A **former friend** was **slightly renowned** in terms of her ability as a non-cook. All she could do was fry—her **fried roast** beef had a reputation (and a life) all of its own. Reputedly it could give hunger a bad name. It also provoked **disciplined gluttony.**

My son recently ordered the **Steak & Ale fish special.** Where have I gone wrong? And would you believe I have an editor who has a **90-minute lunch hour?** Picky, picky.

Army food, Navy food, Air Force food, et al. run together under the rubric of **cafeteria food,** qualifying as either **semi-true** oxymorons or **true semi-quasi** oxymorons. I'm **certainly not sure** which. Not to worry; it's the **same difference.**

Finally, an endearing if not enduring oxymoron came up recently when I **purposely discovered instant espresso—decaffeinated**! I'll have four cups, please—I don't need the sleep.

Feel your favorite food or health oxymoron has been inappropriately slighted? Go ahead, make my day; use the mailer on pages 95—preferably at **your convenience** yesterday.

Versailles, Indiana

From East Chicago, Indiana, to Atlanta, Texas, by Way of Evanston, Wyoming: Geographic Oxymorons

*I*n one of the **old Mary Tyler Moore** shows, Ted Baxter, preparing for a trip to our nation's capital, asks his newsroom colleagues, "Was Washington, D.C., named after the president or the state?" Presumably he still doesn't know (and we still don't care); however, in many ways, the following geographic oxymorons are in the same league as that prophetic, apocryphal question. Thanks, Ted; you needed that.

I was raised in a small but filthy steel town in northwest Indiana, the name of which was (and may even still be) **East Chicago, Indiana.** It was a tough town. How tough was it? When I was a kid, things were so tough we used to go to Gary for vacations—and I looked forward to it. And if you don't think **Gary vacation** is a true oxymoron, you'll probably struggle with **greater Houston** and **downtown Detroit**—and deserve it. First prize is one week in **Miami, Missouri** (Miami, Missouri?), second prize is two weeks . . .

Anyway, my **former hometown,** aside from being a **wretchedly great** place from which to come (it beat staying), is a geographic oxymoron. I really didn't used to mind it when people thought that East Chicago was in Illinois (or that my wife's hometown, **Michigan City, Indiana,** was in Michigan); that made a certain amount of sense, I guess.

But what does bother me, even after **almost exactly** twenty years of living in Atlanta, Georgia, is that when I tell people I am from Atlanta, they reply with "Georgia?" Then it gets through my relatively thick skin (not head), and I respond with "Do you know another Atlanta?" Without exception, they allow they do not. They give up too soon, too easily. It turns out there is another Atlanta. There is indeed an **Atlanta, Texas,** an **Atlanta, Indiana,** and . . .

As a matter of fact, there is a veritable cartographer's twilight zone just around every corner (please, not a **round corner**). While this **real-life** condition may somewhat dilute **mail delivery** as a true oxymoron, the fact remains: Geographic oxymorons abound in this land.

These geographic oxymorons are organized **somewhat differently** from the other units. I have organized them around three **relatively distinct,** although **comparatively unique,** oxymoron forms. The first group comprises cities whose names come from other countries (and beyond), which, when combined with their locations in this country, suggest, minimally, culture shock: for example, **Versailles, Indiana** (the Palace shows movies?). The second group consists of combinations forming **state cities:** for example, **Indiana, Pennsylvania.** And the final group includes jarring and unexpected combinations of city and state: for example, **Orlando, Oklahoma.** The fourth group is made up of city/state pairs requiring no comment (about which I am **grudgingly anxious** to comment).

Culture shock! Do you suppose Julius Caesar would have felt more than just a tad awkward in **Rome, Georgia** (I mean, dressed like that and all), or any more at ease in **Rome, New York**?

I am **slightly intrigued** with **Stuttgart, Arkansas.** Imagine Raymond Massey, in full dress uniform (*mit* Iron Cross), conducting the interrogation, fixing the prisoner in his monocled stare: "We have ways to make you talk—and incidentally, do you still have relatives living in Arkansas?" Following are a few more of this particular form of geographic oxymoron:

Avon by the Sea, New Jersey
Manila, Utah
Norway, South Carolina
Sebastopol, Mississippi
Ceylon, Minnesota
Calais, Maine
Eden, Texas

It has been suggested two reasons why postage rates keep going up are that the **postal service** is obligated to deliver mail to such faraway places as **Venus, Texas; Moon, South Carolina; Jupiter, Florida;** and **Mars Hill, Indiana** (a **somewhat awesome,** however inconvenient, suburb of **Mars, Pennsylvania**).

My **educated guess** is that it gives every mailman (and that includes **female mail-men**) at least a **minor fit**—or **quite possibly** a **slight hernia**—when they hear about **Nevada, Ohio.** And place these true cartographic oxymorons, if you will/can:

Wyoming, Ohio
Oregon, Missouri (not to be confused with Oregon, Wisconsin)
Oregon, Wisconsin (to be confused with Oregon, Missouri)
Florida, New York
Kansas, Alabama
Carolina, Rhode Island
New England, North Dakota

Are there no such things as states' rights? Where are the boundaries of good taste—not to include the boundaries of good states?

However, the geographic oxymorons that really confuse me (and maybe even the former Perry Mason) are the cases of the misplaced cities. I am a **relatively well-traveled** individual, having been out of my home county on several occasions, even returning on a few; but when I heard about **Boston, Kentucky,** I was **systematically disoriented.** What reaction do you suppose you would get if you were to order scrod at the local diner? On the other hand, I'll bet their basketball team is competitive.

I often worry about **Princeton, Indiana.** If the rest of the Ivy League knew . . . On the other hand, I bet their basketball team is competitive too.

Fort Bragg, California? Don't tell the 82nd Airborne Division! And do you really believe there is such a place as **Kansas City, Missouri**—or **East St. Louis, Illinois**? How about **Missouri City, Texas**?

How would you like to wake up in **Evanston, Wyoming,** after a tough night out with the boys and/or girls? It's a long commute to the **Northwestern campus** (even assuming a **parking place**); it might even drive the **WCTU to drink**. Or, conversely, you wake up one morning to find yourself in **Denver, Pennsylvania.** That would **almost certainly** require a phone call to the motor club. But don't tell them where you are (you probably couldn't get here from there anyway).

Oh, **that** Miami.

Having exposed **Atlanta, Texas,** fairness demands I reveal **Dallas, Georgia.** However, regardless of what you might have heard, it was not the site of the 1984 Republican National Convention. And speaking of that, I recently received a letter from a **former student** who now lives in **Louisville, Colorado**—where the Derby will not be run this year, again—for the third time.

The following might get your **Express Mail** representative delivered in a plain brown rubber jacket:

El Paso, Illinois

Baltimore, Ohio

Anchorage, Kentucky

East Texas, Pennsylvania

Hershey, Nebraska (the city, not the bar)

Savannah, Missouri

Waco, Kentucky

One can only assume **St. Paul, North Carolina,** is (way) across the river from **Minneapolis, Kansas** (swim for it, Mary). And if you are still not aware of it, there's an **Augusta, Kansas.** Do you think the Master's Golf Tournament will ever be the same? Talk about a long drive!

There is indeed a **Transylvania, Louisiana,** presumably with a dawn curfew—drink up, last round! And do you share my difficulty visualizing Pete Rose hustling into (and then out of) **Cincinnati, Iowa**?

You'll be excited to learn there are a Charlottesville and a Mount Vernon in Indiana, while there is a Monticello in Georgia. Do you suppose that upsets Mr. Jefferson, as well as G. Washington?

North, South Carolina, is a **well-kept secret.**

I wonder if Clint Eastwood knows about **Carmel, New York**? **Carmel, Indiana**? And worse, if he finds out, do you think he'll run them out of town?

Candor, New York (that's always been my experience). And you'll be **moderately**

excited to learn there is **little or no truth** to the rumor one must dress formally at all times in **Tuxedo, Maryland.**

Saratoga, Wyoming?

You'll be **slightly devastated** to know there is a **Beverly Hills, Missouri,** presumably moved east by Jed Clampett et al. And I don't know about you, but I can't quite conjure up Harry Truman coming home to **Independence, California.** Give it to 'em, Harry!

Brooklyn, Mississippi (multiple gasps)! Do you think Dixie Walker knows?

There is indeed a **Lake Placid, Florida,** where, arguably, the skating competition involves the Australian crawl. The folks in Cleveland, Ohio, will be pleased to know some folks in Tennessee, Georgia, and Florida, inter alia, share their name—if not their fate.

Galveston, Indiana, ought to bring a few shudders to the weary traveler. ("Gulf Coast" there refers to a gasoline alley.)

How would you like your daughter and/or son to tell you he/she was going to Vassar? And you wrote them in **Poughkeepsie, Arkansas**—and she/he kept answering?

For those who thought Newark was somewhere near the Big Apple, come all the way out west (to Ohio). Or how about the following:

Buffalo, Oklahoma
Dayton, Nevada
St. Paul, Oregon
Phoenix, New York

Some city/states form **pure quasi** geographic oxymorons. Consider **Union City, Georgia; Magnolia, Delaware; Enigma, Georgia** (I'm **definitely undecided**); **Normal, Illinois.** Also get a fix on the following:

Flasher, North Dakota (kinda makes you wonder, but in any event
bring your own raincoat and/or umbrella)

Money, Mississippi (So that's where it is!)

Wisdom, Kentucky (no comment and/or gulp!

Intercourse, Pennsylvania (a declarative statement, a question,
an evaluation, and/or a command?)

Virgin, Utah (a population implosion?)

Racine, Ohio (and Groucho Marx thought it was only a small poet in Wisconsin!)

Humble, Texas (no comment)

Harvard, Nebraska (not to be confused with the beet and/or college of the same name)

Old Town, Maine (I'll bet)

Unity, Maine (wanna bet?)

Peculiar, Missouri (you'll have to show me)

Union, Mississippi (come *on!*)

Blessing, Texas (cannot be improved upon)

Nixon, New Jersey (expletive erased)

And even Benjamin Franklin would acknowledge his most recent issue before acknowledging **Philadelphia, Mississippi.** One **cheese steak,** please; hold the grits—very carefully!

What does **Akron, Alabama,** do for and/or to you? How about **Camden, Alabama**? And **Cuba, Alabama**? (As in the ill-fated CIA operation the Bay of Barbecue?)

It's a geographic jungle out there! Perhaps we are just flat-out running out of names for our cities. Therefore I propose cities be numbered—but given **ZIP names.**

Admittedly, there are other types of geographic oxymorons than those I've already given. For example:

Southern hospitality

Yankee ingenuity

The Great Northwest

Western fashion

Texas chic

country charm

Iowa City

greater Omaha

downtown Los Angeles

But I'm not going to present these quasis here.

Sufficiently systematically disoriented? Ready to throw in the map and/or towel? Has your favorite geographic oxymoron gone undiscovered? If so, avoid the rush, plan your oxymoronic itinerary now by way of the mailer on page 95. And as the former Walter Cronkite used to say, "You are here."

*T*here is a concept in **consumer psychology** (a **consistently eclectic** discipline) suggesting some consumers are innovators, while the balance (presumably the **smaller half**) are adopters. Innovators are on the cutting edge; adopters follow the leaders. I figure I am about two groups behind the adopters.

My friends, neither of whom agreed to—or could—read this book, refer to me as **excitingly plain** (I'm flattered). Other people describe me as having an **underwhelming personality** (I think they give me too much credit). Students (as contrasted to people) refer to me as Dr. Dull (but you have to understand, students polarize about me—either they dislike me intensely or they hate me).

Anyway, it seems to me every time I find a **worthwhile product,** or even one I like, that product becomes **new, improved**—probably on the basis of **marketing research.** Mark Twain was right: "Life is just one damned thing after another"—although I think I **might definitely** challenge that particular order.

An oxymoronic adage in marketing suggests that half of all advertising is effective—unfortunately nobody knows which half. That's **probably true.** While that marketing insight certainly does not qualify as a **new cliché,** it probably is as much **truth in advertising** as exists. In addition, as a **famous anonymous** philosopher once said, "We study history in order to forget it." If he had known about media and marketing, she would have been **less anonymous.** (Do you ever wonder about **modern his-**

New, Improved?
The Media and Marketing Share of the Oxymoron Market

59

tory? One of my better students recently found not only the library, but a **scholarly journal** entitled *Current History.* Funny how time passes when you're being had.)

Anyway, in an era of **small Cadillacs, big Volkswagens, foreign cars built domestically, domestic cars built in other countries, performance sedans,** and **Mercedes trucks,** I get **distinctly addled.** And things like **designer water** and **designer jeans** get to me. And **gentlemen's jeans** are in a lack of class all by themselves. I recently bought a pair of gray Levi's (**gray blue jeans**?); but I rarely wear them because I'm so confused. Let the marketeers shape my **impersonal opinion**!

There's an ad on local radio about **pure .999** silver. While all horses look alike to me, I suspect that is a true oxymoron. A recent Jules Feiffer play broadcast on the Arts & Entertainment Network was touted as being **savagely witty.** It's okay with me; but it's nowhere near the **informative programming** offered by the television announcer who indicated our president had handled himself with **presidential majesty.** Long live the king—and may he wave.

I was recently offered a **full price discount.** I took two—and said thank you.

One day I received an excited phone call at my office from my son—he had obtained a can of **new old Coke.**

I suppose I'm old for my age (or perhaps for any age—with the possible exception of the Dark Ages), but I miss those movie previews from the forties and fifties that used to get my complete attention by **shyly announcing,** "They're back together again for the first time." Pass the popcorn, please.

And would you take a **short break** for the following **commercial messages**?

within budget
public service

White-collar boxing

beyond excellence
associate producer
television talent
public television
taped live

The other day an **entertaining newscaster** talked about the president's having a **vacation routine.** I don't know about you, but if I were *ever* to take a vacation, even a **family vacation** . . .

It is **relatively unimportant** to note this is not the same **fairly informed newscaster** who described a politician as being **extremely middle of the road**—but not a **sincere compromiser.**

One of our local TV stations shows movies termed **encore debuts.** I suppose there is a first time—or even a next time—for everything.

There was a blurb on network TV news recently about **white-collar boxing. I semi-seriously** doubt this will precipitate another Boxer Rebellion (which, to the best of my **limitless knowledge,** was what gave jockey shorts a significant **market share**).

About 127th on my **brief list** of all-time favorite oxymorons is a sportscaster's description of a team as being "predictably unpredictable." *Time* magazine, reporting on the St. Paul, Minnesota, ice festival, described one ice sculpture as a "secular cathedral" (an oxymoronic clerical error?).

In terms of news reporting, call me old-fashioned (or martinied, for that matter), but I have trouble with wars—**civil wars, holy wars, limited wars** (particularly **limited nuclear wars**). And as for **war games** . . .

War games

A television station in Atlanta, during a campaign to revitalize its image and/or increase its market share, used the theme "a new tradition"—so what's old?

Delta Airlines has a car rental arrangement called **Delta Wheels.** Were Bette Davis to hear about it, I suppose she would recommend we fasten our **seat belts** inasmuch as we're going to be in for a bumpy ride. (That's about all, Eve.) And if you wear a seat belt, you must be built very strangely. Perhaps this is a sample (or all) of **engineering humor.**

And no media and marketing oxymoron list would be complete without the marketing classic **genuine imitation**—or is it **real imitation**?

Well, sweetheart, that's the way the oxymoronic cookie crumbles. Did your favorite media and marketing oxymoron get canned? No big thing; merely rip off the mailer on page 95—no purchase of proof necessary.

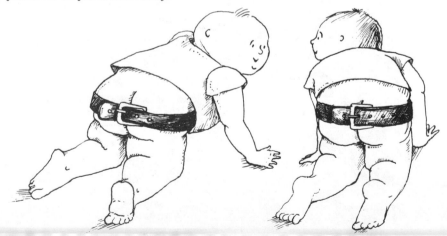

Seat belts

Most **concerned citizens** remember their first interaction with government—perhaps obtaining a **Social Security** card. However, I'm **fairly certain** my **most vague memory** is of when I was a bright but conscientious undergraduate student—in particular, between my junior and senior years when I spent a **short summer** as a **laid-back ROTC cadet** at Fort Campbell, Kentucky.

Of all the charming, fulfilling, whimsical, fun, erudite, madcap, intellectual things we did that summer, one of my **least fond** memories of my **military career** yet to come was the first morning. Somewhere before dawn and death, a **wonderfully vulgar, beautifully acned,** charmingly accented **gentleman** of tremendously low rank (whose hate for us **college men** was exceeded only by his abhorrence, detestation, loathing, disdain, abomination, scorn, and/or deprecation) **fell us out.** Slightly beyond the top of his **pubescent voice,** he **casually screamed,** "Awright, you **unsung heroes**"—Even *he* knew about oxymorons before I did! That really smarts!—"line up **alphabetically according to height**!"

We tried and tried! (After all, we were to become **junior officers.**) And I **still believe,** had it not been for a semi-total eclipse of the sun that night, we just might have done it. Anyway, that was **my impersonal** introduction to government. Following are some of my **subsequent introductions.**

Federal Assistance
and Other
Oxymorons from
the Halls
of Government

"Line up alphabetically according to height."

Breathes there a **served citizen** who does not understand **federal assistance, postal service,** and/or **military intelligence** all qualify as, minimally, true oxymorons. No doubt **minor recognition** will be forthcoming, inasmuch as the **federal budget** has recently been resolved—along with the **civil service** concerns. Where do we line up?

Pending **congressional agreement**—or even **congressional approval**—debate the following:

United Nations

tax reform

(how about **meaningful tax reform**?)

city association

moderate extremist

tax return

public service

And I propose we vote on whether **political party** is or is not a true or a quasi oxymoron.

I couldn't make up my mind whether to include this next oxymoron here or with the media and marketing contradictions. Were you as **negatively impressed** as I was when, during "Baby Doc" Duvalier's **planned exodus,** the news media **fairly consistently** referred to him first as the "president for life" and then ultimately as the—are you ready?— "former president for life"? As an **informed citizen,** I figured I must have missed something.

Political party

An **international politician** was recently characterized as a **moderate rightist.** Okay, if you say so. What say you to these?

voter turnout

citizen soldier

high school civics

political speech

legal language

volunteer army

Probably not unlike you, I get **personal form letters** from my Washington representative(s). Should I believe what I **almost hear** and **almost read**? Is he/she really **strong on weakness**? **Weak on strength**? **Somewhat for this**? And/or **definitely (with qualification) against that**? Does she/he have **my interests** at heart? **Your interests**? **Any interest**? (Any heart?)

Political oxymoron? A wheel within a wheel? Or a deal within a deal? **Balanced budget** is a true oxymoron to our elected officials.

You may recall the United States Supreme Court gave us the classic **deliberate speed.** And in another country that shall go nameless, political dissidents were recently offered **partial amnesty**—I presume they accepted most of it.

I **firmly believe** there are **two bottom lines** to this oxymoronic category. The first is **political promise;** and the second (still) is "Line up alphabetically according to height." If you choose to contribute a government oxymoron, fill out the form on page 95—two copies in triplicate; retain the **original copy** for your files.

Balanced budget

My **academic training** at Indiana University (no doubt an oxymoron to the good folks in West Lafayette) and Purdue University (even less doubt an oxymoron to the equally good folks in Bloomington) was in science, albeit behavioral science, psychology. I didn't start out in psychology. (Does anyone?) I started out to become an English professor. However, for a variety of **semi-good** reasons I switched majors.

Those reasons included the **somewhat assumed fact** I didn't look good in tweed jackets. It later turned out I also didn't look good in **herringbone jackets** (even with real herring bones), **solid jackets,** plaid jackets, or checked—or even unchecked—jackets. I was told English professors don't make much money. (It also later turned out management professors don't make much money, psychology professors don't make much money, professor professors don't make much money, etc.)

In addition, my handwriting was somewhat atrocious, if not nonexistent altogether. We once had a poorest-handwriting contest at the office. I came in first, second—and tied for third. I knew I could win the contest if only someone could read my entry. Also, my spelling were almost as well as my grammer (yet another reason to go into **professional writing**— maybe even an **unwritten law**).

And I mumbled (but only when I spoke, I countered weakly).

Perhaps obviously, for these reasons I not only went into psychology, but decided to **kind-of write** this **slightly sensational, tastefully tacky, moderately obscene, nearly perfect, sort-of book**—if I can find the **spare time.**

However, I digress somewhat. These oxymorons deal with science—primarily **social science** and **behavioral science,** because that is my academic background. However, they also deal with statistics, physics, and/or geology (my son's major(s)—this week), and science in general. You will recognize oxymorons from other areas of science as well. I will resist the **creatively trite** oxymoron **science fiction.**

What I find **mildly fascinating** about scientific oxymorons is that initiated scientists perceive them as true oxymorons—or worse, understand them. Consider, for example, **constant variable, standard deviation,** and **statistical proof.** To the uninitiated (a **mere majority** of 99% + of the general population), these are quasi oxymorons. What do **artificial life, negative velocity, artificial intelligence,** and **zero pounds** do to you?

Idle curiosity qualifies, as do **unbiased opinion, partial closure,** and **potentially critical.**

I'd like to see your work-up on the following:

grossly underestimated

broad specialization

unstable trend

vague definition

initial results

beyond limits

Reading **research reports** is **scientific art.** For example, you must be able to understand the intended, and unintended, meaning(s) of such terms as **rational faith,** or a computer program **partially debugged,** or **action plan,** or **linear curve**—as well as **countless numbers** of others. And I forget (if I ever knew) which discipline is an **exact science.** However, it **certainly probably** includes these terms.

negative relationship
research administration
initial deadline
successful replication
research program
normal variance

Statistical language is unto itself (would that it were). For example, **casual investigation** of **forced choice, systematic variance, true negative, straightforward logic, partial success, rater reliability, replicated research,** and **planned research** would be **somewhat revealing.** "Statistical regression" is not an oxymoron. What does **negative selection** do to you? I'm still working on **at or beyond infinity.**

Scientific American?

Having done **more than my share** of research paper presentations, I know **interesting paper** probably proves to be either a true or a quasi.

All know the **relative importance** of conducting **definitive research** by building in as much **anticipated serendipity** as the **research budget** will permit. Opportunities like **first conclusions, precise vagueness,** and **curvilinear relationships** are critical—albeit **beyond perfection**—in the development of a productive research program. Well-done research is often a thing of **grotesque beauty.**

Sunshowers

And let's raise a temperature to the meteorologists, who gave us **partly sunny** (as distinguished from **partly cloudy**), and whose **somewhat attainable** goal in life is to generate a **weather forecast**—preferably an **accurate weather forecast**—and, one hopes, one that does not include **sunshowers** and/or **thundershowers**.

Do you feel that **perfect research** is almost as **phenomenally common** as loose jeans? Or that this unit of scientific oxymorons was **slightly deficient**? Submit your own research proposal (see page 95), and an **objective peer review** will be undertaken.

Light opera

Light Opera
and Other Arts
and Entertainment
Oxymorons That
Will Keep You Awake

I am hardly an **enlightened yuppie**—having moved to Atlanta (Georgia) from the city. As a matter of fact, I may even be **obediently heretical** in my tastes, not going along with what no one else seems to like. **True enough,** from time to time I have been described as a nonconforming conformist. The other day I wondered why this might be.

A thought **slowly leaped** to mind. My family has an old television set—one of only two steam-operated sets on our block (at least, of which I have **indirect knowledge**). But no, it couldn't be that, inasmuch as I was one of the first to point out that television **miniepics** and **miniseries** were oxymorons. True or quasi?

Also, I agree that **light opera** is a true oxymoron; **rock music** is exceeded only by **soft rock;** and **jazz violin** throws me altogether. I have yet to make up my closed mind about the **false veracity** of the **unspoken suggestion** of many that **Boy George** is an oxymoron.

And regretfully, I essentially agree with a report in *Time* magazine that Joan Rivers is the **former permanent guest host** of the **Johnny Carson Show.**

Movie titles offer considerable **oxymoronic comfort.** Consider, for example, these **fairly recent classics:**

Back to the Future

Mr. Mom

Down and Out in Beverly Hills

The Tender Trap
Ordinary People
The Longest Yard
Father Goose
Rocky II

There's a movie whose advertising **modestly proclaims,** "It's the **coolest heat** you'll ever feel." Also, the ad **cautiously trumpets,** it's **"below Miami,** and above the law." Whatever.

And, if the few people I know are any indication, *Oklahoma Crude* probably does not qualify as an oxymoron (or maybe it does).

You may have your favorite movie oxymoron, but for anyone who really understands the **military system,** *An Officer and a Gentleman* comes in first, second, third, and ties for fourth (with *Oh God, You Devil* and/or *Little Big Man*.) Okay, so *Garbo Talks* (but not to me).

Some people would also argue the **TV movie** *The Rosemary Clooney Story* to be an oxymoron, and I am **almost persuaded** that a recent **John Wayne Film Festival** qualifies (right behind the **Randolph Scott Film Festival**). Hot popcorn, nurse—and plenty of it!

Now that television has been established as **more than a semipermanent fad,** attention must be paid to it. **Miss Piggy**? You bet! *Hollywood Squares*? You bet, I guess. **Television programming** and/or **educational television**? **Very likely probably so.**

There was a delightfully oxymoronic flavor—albeit **obviously subtle**—to the **old Mary Tyler Moore** show: Ted Baxter, **authoritative stupidity;** Murray Slaughter, **articulate inexpression;** Rhoda Morgenstern, **eastern Midwest;** Lou Grant, **tough tenderness;** Georgette Franklin, **meek strength;** and Sue Ann Nivens, **domestic**

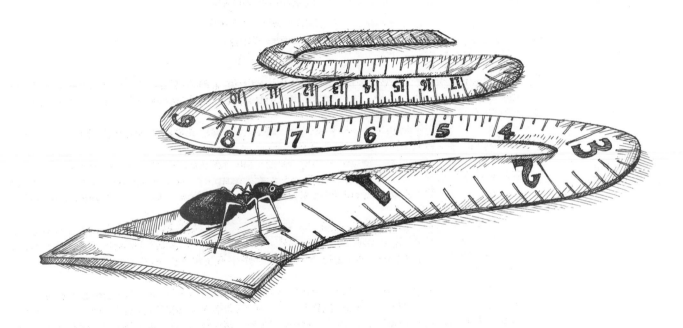

The longest yard

promiscuity. And even a **curable romantic** such as myself has more than a **little difficulty** in even saying **"old Mary Tyler Moore** show." Point me toward the reruns, please.

Also recall that television gave us **stop action** and **instant replay.** I suspect some would argue that *TV Guide* should be included in this **partially complete** list.

Recently someone suggested to me that **Bob Hope special** qualified as an oxymoron, but as a **respectful iconoclast,** I **actively abstained.**

I like music; someone should write some. There are, however, some delightful oxymoronic lyrics. "I Left My Heart in San Francisco" **strongly suggests** Paris is somehow **sadly gay.** In lyrics of the music in the film *Monte Walsh,* someone has "both feet **planted firmly in midair.**"

You may **vaguely remember** the old tune **"Alone Together."** (I often feel that way—but then, I often am.) **"The Lady Is a Tramp"** is no slouch either.

I've already committed myself on **jazz violin,** but consider the following:

rock opera
pianoforte
moderately loud (mf)
simple meter
jazz orchestra
moderately soft (mp)
symphonic band

I'm still old enough to remember when **acid rain** was an oxymoron; therefore, I have at least minor difficulty dealing with **acid rock** et al. However, I think **rock group names** have contributed some delightful oxymorons. Consider, y'know, like, I mean, really:

Soft Cell
The Grateful Dead
Iron Butterfly
Martini Ranch
Led Zeppelin (sic, very; and no doubt the illegitimate cousin-in-law
of the proverbial, however apocryphal, **lead balloon,**
which I still believe will go over, like)
Art of Noise
Violent Femmes
Rubber Rodeo
Electric Light Orchestra
Rain Parade
Dancing Hoods
Fine Young Cannibals

An **oxymoron contributor** recently sent me a brochure describing two brothers, performing musicians, described as a **three-piece duo.** (I'm not sure if that referred to their clothing, their musical instruments, or their repertoire; the only thing of which I am **relatively sure** is they were brothers—the elder being six months younger than his somewhat confused sibling.

I'm still working on **The Fifth Dimension.**

There have been some book titles with oxymoronic quality. My all-time favorite is the Jack Douglas book *My Brother Was an Only Child.* However, I think these deserve either **studied indifference** and/or **riveted inattention:**

The Good War
A Moveable Feast
Family Secrets
The Lonely Crowd
A Paler Shade of White
The 50-Minute Hour
The Golden Age of B Movies
A Perfect Spy

And thanks, Charlie Brown, for **good grief;** we needed that.

Anyway, "fine arts" happily is still a non-oxymoron (**gross arts**?). And the occasional **thunderous silence** or **silent cacophany** about which we all like to complain may indeed be a **false positive**—as opposed to a **true negative.** The arts are indeed alive and well—but hiding out. Unhappily, however, it is the case **crowded museums, crowded libraries,** and **crowded art galleries** are trues.

If you really believe in your heart of arts that your favorite arts and entertainment oxymoron has been **inadequately showcased** here, take it on the road—use the mailer on page 95 to become a patron of the oxymoronic arts. Contribute; give until it hurts. (**Silent scream**?)

As an industrial-organizational psychologist, job titles and occupations naturally interest me professionally, but lately they have become **almost fascinating.** Before you think I am **clearly confused,** let me remind me this unit deals with occupational oxymorons.

Psychologists have a variety of reputations—**all well-deserved,** and **completely accurate.** For example, when my wife and I go to a party, I **almost always** try to find an interesting book, turn my back to the world, and read until she taps me on the shoulder (if I'm lucky) and **insistently suggests,** "Dear, it's time to go home." If I've had a nice time, I more often than not thank the **absentee host and/or hostess.** Therefore, I am particularly fond of, and can identify with, **social psychologist.**

An inordinate number (greater than zero) of my friends are lawyers. I submit **legal brief** is a true oxymoron; you be the judge. However, demonstrating excessive professional maturity, courtesy, and self-restraint, I will forgo **criminal lawyer,** however grudgingly.

I watch television about **25 hours daily**—more on weekends if I can adjust my **light schedule.** I am particularly addicted to sports—any sport. Recently, while **semi-watching** a horse race, I heard one rider described as a **tall jockey.** I figured it was time to have either my hearing or my television checked. Given that physicians work cheaper than **television repair** people, I went in for my **third annual** physical of the year. (Incidentally, the term **"medical practice" slightly concerns** me.)

In terms of **vocational counseling,** strange things can happen. I've heard of **squeamish hematologists, clumsy jugglers, acrophobic mountain-climbers, tone-deaf musicians, talented rock stars, dull acupuncturists.** . . .

Anyway, here are some occupational oxymorons, **give or take** a few. I hope my colleagues and friends (both of them) will recognize themselves:

I do a reasonable amount of traveling; but I am not yet too sophisticated to enjoy touring and sightseeing. Unfortunately, **articulate tour guide** and **informed tour guide** don't show and tell me much. What does **relaxing tour** do to and/or for you?

Few would argue that **anemic vampire** is—or is not—an oxymoron. And how does **virgin prostitute** grab you? (I suppose we all have to start somewhere.) **Timid boxer**? **Forthright diplomat**? Trues or quasis?

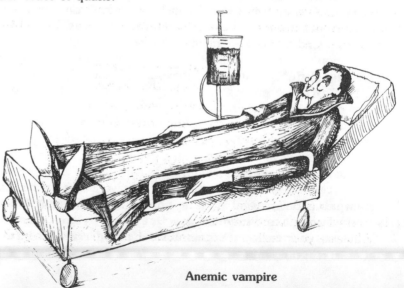

Anemic vampire

Work on these occupational oxymorons:

silent barber

loquacious librarian

military adviser

working relationship (I know it doesn't belong here, but I like it)

modest stripper

moderate terrorist

As an **overpaid professor,** I totally suspect **prepared student** to be an oxymoron—not unlike **graduate student.** Incidentally, my teaching colleagues **are** underpaid—and that's **too much money.** I have a friend who is a **child psychiatrist.** One might but wonder. Also but wonder about these:

subjective scientist

objective lawyer

self-effacing artist

shy bartender

secure advertising executive

cheerful undertaker

clumsy surgeon

I am somewhat blessed to have a **personable accountant**—who makes house calls—and a **compassionate editor.**

What are your feelings about **practical nurse**? **Fast waiter**? **Cabin attendant**?

Shy bartender

Frankly, I get **positively anxious** when I hear about a **scientific writer** (**scientific writing**?) or a **sad clown.** The credits for the television show *M*A*S*H* include a category called **creative consultants.** The mind boggles, boggles, bog . . .

The English Parliament houses a whole class of people with an oxymoronic title—the **Loyal Opposition.** One oxymoronic occupation we all have in common is **Dear Occupant.**

And before you tell me, I'll tell you: **oxymoron expert.** I know, I know.

Those who live in the city (**city life**?) know **parking lot attendant** for the oxymoron it is. Having **relatively nothing** to do with that, my father, now **retired again,** thought of

Baby doctor

himself as a **painless dentist.** And, given **numb patients,** he **certainly might** have been right. Even so, scrape away on these:

gentleman farmer

baby doctor

former Nazi

commercial artist

managing editor

Playboy bunny

And no, I didn't forget the classic oxymoron **civil engineer.** (One—at least this one—can only hope this will be read to them. **Verbal symbols**?)

And finally, the **accurate rumors** you heard are **relatively true.** I did **once or twice** campaign with **slothlike vigor** for the office of **managing director** of the local **Recluse Association.** However, I lost the election (yes, a quorum was present) to a candidate who positioned herself toward the **extreme middle** by describing herself as a **gregarious hermit**—probably a **political scientist.**

Once again, has your favorite occupational oxymoron been omitted? Continue not to worry, see page 95, and share that oxymoron just as soon as possible, assuming you are not—as, alas, am I—a **conscientious procrastinator.** And don't give me that ''the oxymoron is in the mail'' stuff.

nd what does it all mean? Well, nothing, I hope—but more on that later.

RECORDS
Many people are devotees of the *Guinness Book of World Records;* I must have been absent that day. However, do you suppose the following are between those particular covers: the world's shortest mile, largest Chihuahua, worst good guy, smallest St. Bernard, longest yard, ugliest beauty, shortest giant, fastest walker, slowest runner (who was just lapped by the world's fastest walker), prettiest monster, thinnest heavy person, nicest terrorist, most orderly scatterbrain, best bad guy, fastest snail, smallest castle, sweetest lemon, heaviest thin person, sourest candy, most ordinary person, nosiest oyster? Okay, so you don't suppose.

NARCOLEPSY CURES
For some reason I get an inordinate number of narcoleptics in my classes. I can deal with it, but I do get embarrassed when I note myself dozing off. During those last few waking moments, in an attempt to hang on, I often try to imagine the sound of one hand clapping, or what nothing looks like, or zero pounds, or a piece of rope so long it has only one end, or more than 100%, or zero inches, or the sound of silence, or (gasp!) **beyond infinity** (certainly a **sure cure**) . . . and sometimes it works.

OXYMORONIC QUOTES

This particular oxymoron book has looked only at oxymorons in the form of pairs of contradictory words (or, occasionally, terms). Be assured there are longer, classic and quotable oxymoronic utterances. My favorite is Groucho Marx's "I wouldn't belong to any club that would have me as a member," although Howard Cosell's "I never made a mistake in my life. Once I thought I did, but I was wrong" pushes Groucho a mite. In a recent performance review, I was criticized by an **anonymous colleague** for "spending too much time with the students." (**Too much time with the students**?) Total guilt; to whom do I apologize?

How many times have you heard, "You can't get there from here"? And it was Don Rickles who once (okay, twice) said, "If I don't dress up like a woman at least once a month, I think I'll go crazy." I have no idea who said, "I'd give my right arm to be ambidextrous"— but I'd like to shake his or her hand. Many have been **accurately inaccurately** quoted as saying, "It's my humility that makes me great."

A major-league baseball player often accused of not giving his all responded with: "The word 'malingerer' is not in my vocabulary. I mean, it's in my vocabulary, but I never *use* it."

And all **too true,** nostalgia is not what it used to be.

And one of my favorite cartoons is the one of the man in the public washroom who stands in front of the mirror on which is written "Give to Mental Health Week or I'll kill you." I'm thinking, I'm thinking.

HEAVY HUMOR

Fortunately or unfortunately, depending on your point of view, I was **totally successful** in accomplishing my intention **not** to make this an intellectual effort (**intellectual oxymoron** perhaps being the **ultimate oxymoron**). My **active abstinence** notwithstanding, if I may

Heavy humor

be permitted one scholarly observation, I am rapidly approaching the **tentative conclusion** that oxymorons are the conceptual basis of all humor. Heavy. (**Heavy humor**?) Enough.

In addition, I have several ideas regarding application of oxymorons to marketing problems, particularly in advertising—but more on that next time.

THE CURSE OF THE OXYMORON

You may have forgotten, but I haven't. The single purpose of this **first annual** oxymoron book was to describe the ubiquitous and insidious nature of oxymorons, to raise your awareness level regarding oxymorons, to infect and/or addict you, TO RUIN YOUR LIFE just as has mine been **somewhat destroyed.** (You don't believe me? Look at page 19.) How am I doing so far?

If anyone got this far, I'm doing **fairly well.** However, here's a test. Ask yourself this question: Will you ever be able to look at another appetizer menu in a fine restaurant without thinking oxymoron? I certainly hope not. (And frankly, I really doubt an appetizer menu exists anywhere with **diminutive whale.** But if so, I'll take two—they're **certainly probably** small.)

If you are not addicted by now (so you're the one), I can attribute your loss only to great character strength, my **delightfully pedantic writing style,** and/or your illiteracy (in this case, functional illiteracy). If I have accurately described you as nonaddicted, from now on please try to continue not to find oxymorons. But if by chance you should run across one or two, share them with the rest of us.

ANTIDOTE FOR THE CURSE OF THE OXYMORON

George Carlin (who has been known to drop a few oxymorons, inter alia) talks about a mysterious illness for which there are no known symptoms and for which there is no known cure. (I may—or may not—have it. I'm not sure; I've been feeling pretty good lately.) Oxymoron addiction (to include oxymoron OD) is easier to treat. I know the symptoms (and you *have* them); it's the cure that throws me. On the other hand, why should anyone want to be cured?

However, fairness demands I give you the antidote. Therefore, now heed this: Studiously avoid situations where people write, read, speak, and/or listen. That's it; that's truth; be well.

PERSPECTIVE

Finally, if you took this whole thing seriously, you missed the point; and I recommend you go back to square one just before reading this. One more time! (You'll just have to do it until you get it right.)

WHAT NEXT? (IS THERE LIFE AFTER OXYMORONS?)

Second, stamp out the forthcoming Stamp Out Oxymorons movement. Then, take an oxymoron to lunch during this, the International Year of the Oxymoron—preferably a **long lunch.** Share it with someone you love (but don't tell your spouse).

And yes, the recurring rumors you hear about me are **essentially true.** I am soon to become an **internationally unknown oxymoron expert, nameless celebrity, instant folk hero, academic sex symbol, oxymoron club franchiser, T-shirt designer,** and **modestly famous;** but I want you to know none of this will deflect me from my new life's goal (this week)—to become the consummate ultimate antepenultimist, or, failing that, the consummate ultimate anti-antepenultimist.

Having now accomplished my former life's goal of ruining your life by way of oxymoron addiction, I once again leave you with this **single thought:**

THINK OXYMORON (CAVEAT EMPTOR, Y'ALL)

. . . and please watch how you pronounce "oxymoron"!

(*Now* can I get back to being an industrial-organizational psychologist again?)

P.S. About the footnote on page 22—how many of the non-boldface oxymorons did you identify correctly?

Wrong!

MAILER: **SECOND DEADLINE**

Had enough? Can't stand it any longer? Grasp pen between thumb and forefinger. Complete the following and **mail to:**

> **Dr. Warren S. Blumenfeld**
> **Internationally Unknown Oxymoron Expert**
> **The Oxymoron Institute of North America (and Georgia)**
> **International Headquarters**
> **P.O. Box 824003**
> **Atlanta, GA 30324**
> **Attention: Jumbo Shrimp and/or New, Improved Products Division**

My most favorite oxymoron was _____
My least favorite oxymoron was _____
Ten oxymorons that were not included, but should have been and probably will be in the next **oxymoron book,** are

	Oxymoron	Source	Category
1.			
2.			
3.			
4.			
5.			
6.			
7.			
8.			
9.			
etc.			

(continued)

My name is   _____

My address is _____

_____

_____

I probably will definitely buy one or more copies of the next **oxymoron book:**

    ____Maybe

    ____Firm maybe

    ____Firmer maybe

    ____Firmest maybe

    ____Unqualified maybe (be less specific, if at all possible, please):

THANK YOU FOR YOUR INTENSE DISINTEREST